THE CIVIL WAR HISTORY SERIES

THE CIVIL WAR ON THE
VIRGINIA
PENINSULA

Private John Moore, an illiterate farmer, was enlisted in Company I (York Rangers) of the 32nd Virginia Volunteers. He was captured at Sharpsburg on September 17, 1862, and later paroled. Moore was also wounded during Grant's Overland Campaign on May 12, 1864.

On the Cover: Officers of the 1st Connecticut Heavy Artillery stand proudly beside their 13-inch seacoast mortars in Battery No. 4 near Yorktown. These 8 1/2-ton siege weapons could send a 220-pound shell 4,300 yards. Union General George McClellan would position 103 siege guns in April 1862 to bombard the Confederate Warwick-Yorktown Line into submission. The Confederates retreated before these guns ever fired a shot.

THE CIVIL WAR HISTORY SERIES

THE CIVIL WAR ON THE VIRGINIA PENINSULA

John V. Quarstein

ARCADIA
PUBLISHING

Published by Arcadia Publishing
Charleston, South Carolina

Printed in the United States of America

Library of Congress Catalog Card Number: 2006941008

For all general information contact Arcadia Publishing at:
Telephone 843-853-2070
Fax 843-853-0044
E-mail sales@arcadiapublishing.com
For customer service and orders:
Toll-Free 1-888-313-2665

Visit us on the Internet at www.arcadiapublishing.com

The Confederate Water Battery at Yorktown was photographed in May 1862.

Contents

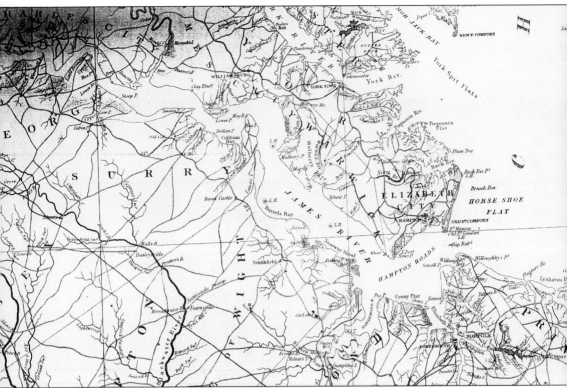

This is Herman Boyle's 1825 map (April 1859 version with corrections), which was based on John Wood's 1819 map of the Virginia Peninsula.

This view shows the arrival of wounded soldiers during the Peninsula Campaign at Fort Monroe's Engineer Wharf, 1862.

Introduction

When Virginia left the Union in April 1861, Northern and Southern leaders alike recognized the Peninsula as an extremely strategic location. The Virginia Peninsula, bordered by the James and York Rivers, was one of two major approaches to the Confederate capital at Richmond. The bountiful, yet strategic waterways, fertile farm fields, and quiet little towns along this path to Richmond would immediately become the scene of some of the Civil War's greatest events.

The key to Union control of the Peninsula was Fort Monroe. Built on Old Point Comfort to command the entry to Hampton Roads, this moat-encircled masonry bastion was the only fort in the Upper South not to fall into Confederate hands when the war erupted. Virtually overnight Fort Monroe became a major base for Federal fleet and army operations.

Brigadier General Benjamin F. Butler arrived at Fort Monroe in mid-May 1861 and immediately strove to expand Union control over the entire Peninsula. His troops quickly occupied and fortified Newport News Point to block Confederate use of the James River. More important, however, to the war's outcome was Butler's May 24, 1861 decision to consider slaves escaping into Union lines as "Contrabands of War." It was the Civil War's first steps toward becoming a war to end slavery, and Fort Monroe became a magnet for African Americans seeking freedom.

The Union presence on the Peninsula was considered obnoxious by the local Confederates. Butler's efforts to move up the Peninsula were stopped by Southerners at Big Bethel on June 10, 1861. It was the Civil War's first land battle. John Bankhead Magruder, the Confederate commander, became an instant Southern hero, but soon took the war to new heights of devastation when he ordered Hampton's destruction. Local Confederate troops burned their hometown on the evening of August 7, 1861, rather than witness its desecration by Northern troops and contrabands.

The battle lines were now drawn across the Peninsula and would remain the same until the spring of 1862, when Union General George B. McClellan conceived his brilliant plan to strike at Richmond by way of the Peninsula. It was a sound concept enabling the Union to utilize its naval superiority to protect McClellan's flanks and carry his troops. Richmond seemed doomed, yet despite all his advantages, McClellan would fail to achieve his objective because of the events that occurred on the lower Peninsula.

Even before McClellan began moving his 121,000 troops to the Peninsula, the emergence of the powerful Confederate ironclad ram C.S.S. *Virginia* (*Merrimack*) disrupted his plan. The *Virginia* sank the wooden U.S.S. *Cumberland* and U.S.S. *Congress* on March 8, 1862. No longer would wooden sailing ships rule the waves; ironclads became the key to naval superiority. The next day, March 9, 1862, the Union ironclad marvel, U.S.S. *Monitor*, appeared in Hampton Roads and dueled the *Virginia* in history's first battle between ironclads. The battle was a draw, but the *Virginia* blocked the James River and forced McClellan to concentrate on the York River.

Waiting for McClellan's massive army was "Prince John" Magruder's small 13,000-man army entrenched along the Warwick River. Magruder bluffed McClellan into believing that the Confederates outnumbered his army, prompting the Union commander to besiege the Warwick-Yorktown Line for four weeks, beginning April 5, 1862. The delay was critical and contributed to the campaign's ultimate downfall.

The main Confederate army, commanded by General Joseph E. Johnston, moved down to the Peninsula in late April, but abandoned the Warwick-Yorktown Line on May 3. Thus, McClellan's elaborately planned assault had no one to destroy. The Union was, however, able to catch up with the retreating Confederates at the old colonial capital of Williamsburg. The May 5, 1862 bloody Battle of Williamsburg enabled the Confederates to continue their escape toward Richmond.

The Peninsula Campaign did result in the Union seizing control of all of the Peninsula. It would remain in Union hands throughout the war, providing a strategic base from which the Federals would launch attacks against other Confederate cities, forts, and ports. When the war ended, Southerners returned to find their homeland devastated and changed forever, while Fort Monroe continued to serve the Union cause as a prison for the former Confederate president, Jefferson Davis.

The Peninsula's Civil War experience is filled with meaningful stories about leadership, valor, sacrifice, freedom, and technology. The forts, earthworks, historic buildings, and battlefields that dot our landscape today remain as testaments to the war that forever changed America.

This view of Warwick Courthouse was sketched by Sgt. Peterman in April 1862. Warwick C.H. was a small community of six buildings and twenty-six residents. During the Peninsula Campaign, Brigadier General Erasmus Darwin Keyes used the small courthouse building as the headquarters for the Union IV Corps. The balloon *Constitution* was deployed in the courthouse green.

One

The Gathering Storm

The Virginia Peninsula is a narrow strip of land formed by the Chesapeake Bay, York River, Hampton Roads, and the James River. Prior to the Civil War the lower Peninsula was home to the small towns of Williamsburg, Yorktown, and Hampton; as well as Elizabeth City, York, James City, and Warwick Counties. George Ben West noted that "No one could desire to live in a more favored place with its mild climate, its delightful and health giving sea breezes, its accessibility both by land and water, made it a most desirable section for a home. It was settled by a happy and contented company of prosperous farmers, with comfortable homes, loving families, well tilled and fertile lands, and loyal slaves, everything to make them free from care." Lee Hall Mansion (pictured here) was built in the 1850s by Richard Decauter Lee, one of Warwick County's wealthiest planters, and it typifies the gentry lifestyle on the Peninsula.

One of the first landfalls made by the English when they arrived in Virginia in 1607 was at a spit of land which would eventually be called Old Point Comfort. Captain John Smith immediately recognized it as a place of extreme strategic importance. Located 20 miles from the Chesapeake Capes and commanding the entrance to Hampton Roads, Old Point Comfort would dominate the Peninsula during the Civil War.

Some officers and their wives posed for this photograph in front of the casemate quarters in Fort Monroe, c. 1861.

Old Point Comfort was first fortified in 1609 with an earthwork named Algernourne Fort. The fort was burned in 1612 and even though other fortifications would follow at different times of military emergency, the Peninsula was virtually defenseless when the British invaded the Chesapeake Bay in 1813. The nearby town of Hampton was burned by troops commanded by Admiral Sir George Cockburn and the British fleet blockaded Hampton Roads until the war was over. The War of 1812 clearly stated the need for fortifications to protect the region. Thus, Congress approved the construction of a masonry fortification on Old Point Comfort.

Named for President James Monroe and designed by the distinguished French military engineer and former aide-de-camp to Napoleon, Brigadier General Simon Bernard, Fort Monroe would become the largest moat-encircled masonry fortification in America. The fort would eventually cover 63 acres with the circumference of its walls being over a mile in length. Construction on the fort began in earnest in 1819 and was virtually complete by 1834.

Fort Monroe was designed to mount 412 guns and to house a wartime garrison of 2,625 officers and men. The fort's design featured seven fronts with several large bastions to maximize direct, flank, and cross-fire. Extensive outerworks, including a redoubt and redan, were built to protect

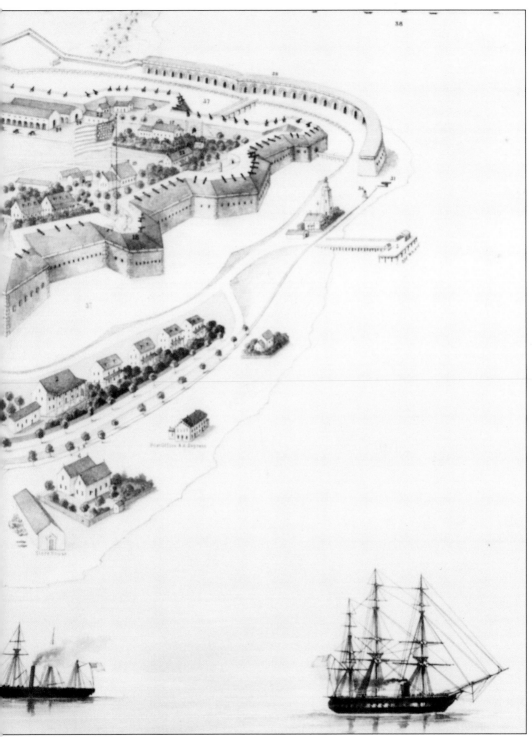

it from land attack. The fort included a Water Battery containing forty guns to concentrate fire at vessels before they could enter the channel.

Fort Monroe soon became one of the most important military installations in the South. In 1824 it was selected as the location of the Artillery School of Practice. The school was established by Brevet Brigadier General Abraham Eustis. The fort also saw active service as an assembly, training, and embarkation site during the Seminole War, the Black Hawk War, and the Mexican War.

Many individuals who later gained rank and acclaim during the Civil War served at Fort Monroe prior to the war. The young engineer Robert E. Lee helped supervise the moat's construction in the early 1830s; his first son, George Washington Custis Lee, was born at Fort Monroe. Others include John B. Wool, Robert B. Anderson, Silas Casey, Samuel Cooper, Joseph E. Johnston, and Jubal Early. This is a view of Headquarters No. 1, which housed the post commander and important guests to the fort such as President Abraham Lincoln in 1862.

14

Fort Monroe's one weakness was that its guns could not totally command the main shipping channel leading into Hampton Roads. A companion work was designed on a shoal known as the Rip-Raps to counter this problem. An artificial island of stone was built and named Fort Calhoun in honor of then-Secretary of War John C. Calhoun. Construction began in 1823, but foundation problems delayed completion until 1860.

Fort Calhoun, often called Castle Calhoun or simply the Rip-Raps, was designed as a tower battery with three tiers of casemates. The fort was supposed to mount 232 guns and house a wartime garrison of 1,130 officers and men. However, when Fort Calhoun neared completion in 1860, it was greatly modified from its original design.

15

Fort Monroe would dominate the Peninsula and Hampton Roads region socially, economically, and politically. The fort's existence made the surrounding communities secure, but soon would become a major thorn in the local citizenry's effort to forge a separate nation. This image is of Hampton native Thomas Marshall Jones. A West Point graduate, Jones served as a lieutenant in the 8th U.S. Infantry prior to 1861. On February 28, 1861, Jones resigned his commission and joined the Confederate army. He served in the Lower South and rose to the rank of brigadier general.

Few Peninsula residents realized in 1861 that within four years their agrarian lifestyle would be destroyed. Soon they would find their homes and fields in ruin, their slave workforce liberated, their financial resources depleted, and their homeland under military occupation. The Civil War would change forever Dr. Humphrey Harwood Curtis's Endview Plantation (pictured here) and with it the entire Virginia Peninsula.

Two

Ben Butler and the Contrabands

The fall of Fort Sumter on April 13, 1861, prompted Virginia to leave the Union on April 17, 1861. The Virginians were quick to capture the Gosport Navy Yard and the Harpers Ferry Arsenal, but were unable to organize any attempt against Fort Monroe. The fort, often called the "Key to the South," had already proven itself as an operations base for points farther south such as Fort Pickens guarding Pensacola, Florida.

Fort Monroe was the only Federal fort to remain in Union hands in Virginia during the secession crisis. The fort's commanding officer in the spring of 1861 was Lieutenant Colonel Justin Dimick, an 1819 West Point graduate. Forty years of military service, including brevets for gallantry in the Seminole War and the Mexican War, had well prepared him for the emergency at hand.

Colonel Dimick focused on strengthening Fort Monroe against any possible Confederate attack. By mid-May, the fort had been reinforced with the 3rd and 4th Massachusetts and the 1st Vermont regiments, numbering over 2,100 men. This is an image of the Hancock Light Guard, 4th Massachusetts Regiment just before its arrival at Fort Monroe.

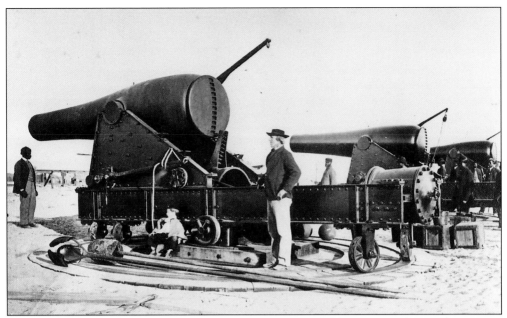

U.S. Army Commander-in-Chief Lieutenant General Winfield Scott noted in mid-May 1861 that "Fort Monroe is by far the most secure post now in the possession of the U.S., against any attack that can be possibly made upon it . . ." Scott believed that the fort would become the Union's major base for operations against the Confederate coast and ports.

The local Confederates had not been idle, as Benjamin Stoddard Ewell, president of the College of William and Mary and an 1832 graduate of West Point, began mobilizing volunteers for the defense of the Peninsula. Yet, he was virtually powerless to block the advance of Federal forces near Fort Monroe into nearby Hampton.

19

Winfield Scott decided that the Union must expand its position on the Peninsula. He selected Major General Benjamin Franklin Butler to assume command of the newly created Union Department of Virginia. Butler, an astute criminal lawyer and pre-war Democratic politician, had already achieved fame when he thwarted the secessionist movement in Maryland.

Union troops had already crossed Mill Creek and established Camp Hamilton, named in honor of Lieutenant Colonel Schuyler Hamilton, Winfield Scott's military secretary. By May 20, it housed the 2nd New York and the 1st Vermont Volunteers. By the time Butler arrived at Fort Monroe, his entire command numbered over 4,451 men and officers.

When the Union troops established Camp Hamilton, they occupied Villa Margaret, the summer home of former President John Tyler. Tyler had recently died and his wife was shocked by the lack of respect shown by the Massachusetts troops for private property. Mrs. Tyler called the invaders, "these scum of the earth," but she was unable to regain her property until the war was over.

One of the more colorful units to arrive at Fort Monroe in late May 1861 was the 5th New York Infantry Regiment, known as Duryee's Zouaves. The unit had been organized by wealthy New Yorker Abram Duryee, who had long been active in his state's antebellum militia. The unit adopted the Zouave uniform style and drill which had been popularized by the French army in Algeria and the Crimea. The Duryee's Zouaves was made up of some of New York's leading citizens. Unit members Gouverneur K. Warren, H. Judson Kilpatrick, Joseph E. Hamblin, and Henry E. Davies eventually became Union generals.

On May 23, Butler decided to send Colonel J. Wolcott Phelps and the 1st Vermont into Hampton. While just a reconnaissance mission, the Confederates were unable to block the Union advance. The Federals closed the local polls, since on that day Virginia voters were to approve the Ordinance of Secession, and then returned to Fort Monroe. The citizens of Hampton were appalled at the Union aggression and overwhelmingly confirmed the Ordinance of Secession. George William Semple, an 1830 graduate of the College of William and Mary, was a pre-war Hampton doctor and enlisted in the Confederate army as a surgeon of the 32nd Virginia Volunteers following this Union aggression.

The Union "reconnoitering expedition" not only proved that the Union could virtually march at will wherever they wished on the Peninsula, but also had far-reaching political implications that changed the Civil War's purpose. Three slaves, owned by Colonel Charles K. Mallory, commander of the 115th Virginia Militia and a pre-war Hampton lawyer, escaped and followed the Union troops to Fort Monroe to secure their freedom.

Colonel Mallory sent Major John Baytop Cary to Fort Monroe to endeavor to obtain the return of his slaves, using the Fugitive Slave Law as justification. Butler, realizing that slavery was at the very core of the conflict and that such laborers were being used to build nearby Confederate fortifications, rejected his request. John Edward Davis was a student at Cary's pre-war Hampton Military Academy and served in the 32nd Virginia Regiment during the war.

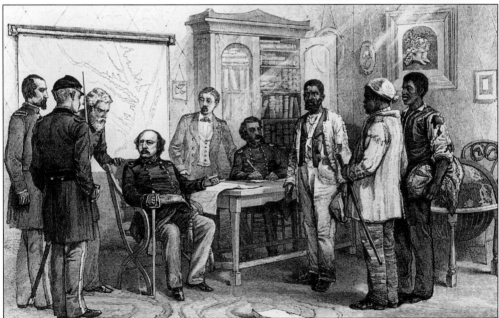

General Butler believed that since Virginia now considered itself independent and that Virginia was at war with the United States, he had no "constitutional obligation" to return the slaves. Butler added that his troops would take possession of whatever property they required. Since slaves were considered "chattel property," Butler called the escaped slaves "contraband of war."

Fort Monroe quickly became a magnet for escaping slaves, and Butler began using them to support Union operations. Numerous blacks took jobs in various military departments with tasks ranging from distribution of food to manual labor at $2.00 a month pay.

In 1861 Abraham Lincoln viewed the Civil War as a conflict to preserve the Union. His objective, politically motivated because of the Border States, was not to disrupt slavery where it existed, but to keep the Fugitive Slave Law in force. Abolitionists disdained this policy and slaves viewed the soldiers in blue as men of freedom. Butler's "contraband of war" decision was the Civil War's first steps toward changing the war's purpose into a conflict about freedom.

Ben Butler had been instructed by Winfield Scott to act with "boldness" in his operations against the local Confederates. Butler strove to contest the construction of Confederate fortifications across Hampton Roads at Sewell's Point, Craney Island, and Pig Point. On May 27, 1861, he sent three regiments of New York, Massachusetts, and Vermont volunteers to occupy Newport News Point in order to blockade the James River.

Butler considered Newport News to be a very strategic site, as he advised Winfield Scott, "The expedition to Newport News . . . landed without opposition. I have caused an entrenched camp to be made there, which, when completed, will be able to hold itself against any force that may be brought against it, and afford an even better depot from which to advance than Fortress Monroe."

"The advantages of the News," Butler wrote, "are these: There are two springs of very pure water there; the bluff is a fine, healthy location. It has two good, commodious wharves, to which steamers of any draught may come up at all stages of the tide; it is as near any point of operation as Fortress Monroe . . ."

"As soon as Colonel Phelps arrived," Private William Osborne of the Fourth Massachusetts recounted, "he began the erection of earthworks. These were of semicircular form, terminating at either extremity on the bank of the river, and were nearly a half mile long. In the ditch in

front of the works were placed obstructions."

Newport News Point was renamed Camp Butler and armed with four 8-inch Columbiads. "On the man works commanding the plain and forest were mounted a number of heavy guns," Private Osborne noted, "while on the bluff facing the river was a battery of five large pieces and among them a Sawyer and James rifle. Upon these works the men . . . labored for many days, and at a time when the weather was extremely hot."

Butler believed that from his new base at Newport News Point he could easily capture the Confederate batteries at Pig Point and Suffolk, thereby severing Norfolk's railroad ties to Richmond, causing that port to surrender. The momentum of success, Butler thought, might even place his troops in a position to capture Richmond.

The Union occupation of Hampton and Newport News Point prompted the local pro-Confederate citizenry to evacuate their homes and move westward toward Williamsburg. Camp Butler quickly became another magnet for escaping slaves and "two large commodious buildings" were erected to house these contrabands. While many contrabands found employment with the Union forces, others became even more inventive oystering and growing crops for sale to Union troops. An informal market was established outside of Camp Butler. Every morning after reveille, blacks would appear from the nearby countryside to sell all sorts of produce, fish, and fowl.

Butler received more men and material enabling him to continue to improve the Federal fortifications. On May 30, 1861, an experimental Sawyer gun was mounted on Fort Calhoun's wharf to shell the Confederate batteries at Sewell's Point.

The Sawyer gun was a rather unsuccessful piece of heavy rifled artillery invented by Sylvanus Sawyer in the mid-1850s. The gun's shell was lead-coated with six ribs casted to its exterior to fit the weapon's rifling. Fort Calhoun's example was a 30-pounder (5.862-inch bore). The Sawyer gun was prone to bursting and sometimes clumsy to load.

Six weeks after the capture of Fort Sumter by Confederate forces, the war on the Peninsula had turned from euphoria into fear for Southern patriots. The bold step toward independence had been crushed on the lower Peninsula and had enabled Ben Butler to move aggressively against Hampton and Newport News Point. The Yankees had indeed come to stay.

The Peninsula society had been turned upside down with the arrival of Union troops. "One cannot help reflecting on the change wrought by time and events," wrote New York Volunteer Captain Ole Peter Balling. "Where now crowds of hardy soldiers refresh their tired frames by gambling in the luxuriously fresh waves of the James River, only twelve months ago the nobility and fashion of the South gathered to enjoy the stillness and beauty of the scenery, and so the change ever goes on! Who knows what sorts of guests may be sojourning at Newport News in August 1862?" The Peachy Family of Williamsburg and their servants typify the Peninsula's antebellum social structure, their lives forever disrupted once "the Yankees came."

Three

The Battle
of Big Bethel

Southern fortunes on the Peninsula appeared at a very low ebb when Colonel John Bankhead Magruder assumed command on May 24, 1861, at Yorktown. Magruder, an 1830 graduate of West Point, was breveted lieutenant colonel for his gallant actions during the Mexican War and was called "a dashing, fearless soldier." Known as Prince John, Magruder was often lauded for high social qualities and fondness for military parades, but his career had been plagued by his heavy drinking. Prince John had his work set out for him.

Magruder quickly set himself to the enormous task of organizing troops and fortifications on the Peninsula. He urged Benjamin Ewell to continue work on building a series of redoubts known as the Williamsburg Line. Slaves and recent recruits, such as George Washington Smith of Cosnahan's Battery, were set to work erecting fortifications.

Butler's aggressions throughout May 1861 had stimulated local Confederate recruitment. On the very day of Butler's occupation of Newport News Point, the enlistment of troops in Warwick County had proceeded under the leadership of twenty-nine-year-old Dr. Humphrey Harwood Curtis of Endview Plantation. Eighty men, including four officers and nine noncommissioned officers (NCOs), were recruited into the "Warwick Beauregards." The unit would eventually become Co. H, 32nd Virginia Infantry.

Men were flocking to the colors throughout the Peninsula, and several companies were organized that would eventually become part of the 32nd Virginia. Recruitment in Williamsburg had begun even before the war. Benjamin Ewell established the Williamsburg Junior Guard. Other units formed in the spring of 1861 included the Wythe Rifles, York Rangers, Hampton Grays, and Nelson Guards. Several artillery units were also organized such as the Peninsula Artillery, Washington Artillery, James City Artillery, and Lee Artillery. Captain Frank Lee organized Company K (Lee Guard) of the 32nd Virginia.

As the local troops were being organized into cohesive units, Magruder sought to create a defensive system which would block any Union advance up the Peninsula. Prince John recognized the major threat posed by the ever growing Union force at Fort Monroe. He decided to play for time by baiting Union General Butler into attacking an advance position. Magruder selected Big Bethel Church as the place to provoke an attack.

Big Bethel Church, located 13 miles below Yorktown and 8 miles from Hampton, seemed to be the best place for the Confederates to establish a forward position. The church was located at a crossroads behind a bend in the northwestern branch (known as Brick Kiln Church) of the Back River. Magruder positioned 1,458 men at Big Bethel, including units commanded by Major Edgar B. Montague, Lieutenant Colonel W.D. Stuart's 3rd Virginia Infantry, and Major George W. Randolph's artillery battalion.

In late May Colonel Daniel Harvey Hill's First North Carolina Volunteers arrived on the Peninsula, and Magruder on June 6, 1861, ordered Hill's regiment to Big Bethel. Hill, a West Point graduate, veteran of the Mexican War, and founder of the North Carolina Military Institute, was placed in overall command of the Confederate position at Big Bethel. He immediately organized the construction of earthworks around Big Bethel and established a forward position 3 miles away at Little Bethel.

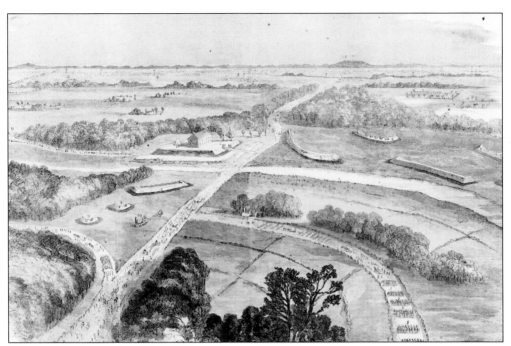

J.W. Ratchford, an aide to D.H. Hill, noted that the Confederates were in a precarious position when he wrote: "It looked as if Magruder was only sending us down to the vicinity of the fort as a dare to General Benjamin F. Butler." Magruder wanted to bring on a fight, hopefully, to defeat the enemy, but also to give himself time to improve his Williamsburg, Yorktown, and Mulberry Island defenses.

D.H. Hill's men constructed earthworks across the northwestern branch of the Back River to defend his right flank, which was also protected by the river and a marsh. One howitzer was added to strengthen this advance position. On the north of Brick Kiln Creek, Hill's troops constructed fortifications which commanded the bridge and encircled the road to defend the position's flanks. Three artillery pieces were placed to control access to the bridge. Also, outside the redoubt a rifled howitzer was positioned to guard a ford.

The Federals, meanwhile, had not been idle. Butler had received additional reinforcements and began probing the surrounding countryside to thwart Confederate troop movements. On June 4, elements of Duryee's Zouaves, the 5th New York (pictured here), marched to the little village of Fox Hill and then returned to Fort Monroe. This action prompted the Confederates to burn Howard's Bridge on the Hampton-York Road to protect their York River flank.

On June 7 and again on June 9, Federal reconnoitering parties, Colonel Max Weber's Turner Rifles, clashed with Confederates near New Market Bridge. D.H. Hill reported to Magruder after the June 9 fight that "reliable citizens reported that two cartloads and one buggy load were taken into Hampton. We had not a single man killed."

Ben Butler now was alert to the increasing Confederate presence near Hampton. The Federal commander believed that he needed to strike out and destroy the Confederate entrenchments at Big Bethel which might open the door to Richmond. Butler conceived a somewhat complex plan to send troops from Camp Butler, Camp Hamilton, and Fort Monroe to converge on the Bethel area before dawn on June 10. The night march was planned to give the Union force, including the Duryee's Zouaves pictured here, an element of surprise which, it was hoped, would help ensure victory.

The Union strike force was placed under the command of Brigadier General Ebenezer W. Pierce. Duryee's Zouaves led the march across Hampton Creek at midnight, to intersect the Confederate positions between Little and Big Bethel. The Zouaves were then followed a hour later by Colonel Frank Townsend's 3rd New York Regiment with two howitzers. Lieutenant Colonel Peter T. Washburn organized men from the 1st Vermont and 4th Massachusetts who were to march from Camp Butler to make a demonstration in front of Little Bethel. Colonel John E. Bendix's 7th New York with two field guns was to follow Washburn from Newport News Point.

Butler's night march plan dictated that Union units should juncture near Little Bethel Church and then march against the Confederate entrenchment. Federal soldiers wore white armbands to distinguish themselves from the enemy in the dark. Yet, when the 3rd New York and 7th New York approached each other, the 3rd New York fired into the ranks of their fellow New Yorkers. The Union incurred eighteen casualties in the confusion. More importantly, the Confederates were alerted to the Federal advance. They abandoned Little Bethel and retreated to their defenses at Big Bethel to await the anticipated Union assault.

The Northern musketry had alerted the Southerners to the Federal advance. They abandoned Little Bethel and fell back to the Big Bethel entrenchments. D.H. Hill now deployed his men for the expected Union assault. Lieutenant Colonel William D. Stuart's 3rd Virginia with one howitzer filled the advance redoubt across the creek. Sharpshooters from the 1st North Carolina were positioned on the southern bank of the creek to the east of the Hampton-York Road. Randolph's Richmond Howitzers manned the three guns in the main redoubt facing the bridge; Major Montague's companies and elements of the 1st North Carolina held the main redoubt. Private Richard Curtis (pictured here) Company A (Wythe Rifles), 32nd Virginia fought at Big Bethel.

Even though the Federals knew that the element of surprise had been lost, General Pierce decided to proceed with the attack. The Union units were somewhat disorganized; however, Duryee's Zouaves opened the battle with a charge against the forward Confederate redoubt. The Zouaves quickly came under heavy Southern artillery fire and fell back. Lieutenant John T. Greble (pictured here) and his battery now arrived and began duelling with the Confederate artillery.

The 3rd New York led the second attack and moved to envelop the Confederate right as the 5th New York and 2nd New York marched across the field directly toward the redoubt. The 3rd Virginia abandoned the earthwork under pressure by the New Yorkers. The Union advantage, however, was quickly lost. Colonel Townsend, believing his men were about to be flanked, ordered a withdraw. This enabled a Confederate counter-attack to retake the advanced redoubt.

As the New Yorkers fell back, Major Theodore Winthrop organized an assault against the Confederate left flank using Vermont and Massachusetts troops. The Union soldiers crossed the creek with a loud cheer under a withering fire. Winthrop, rallying his men for a final charge, stood on a log brandishing his sword and was immediately shot through the heart. His death demoralized his troops and they retreated. "This withdrawal," wrote Confederate D.H. Hill, "decided the action in our favor."

Major Winthrop and Lieutenant Greble, who was killed at the end of the battle while serving his cannon, were lionized for their valor and sacrifice. Greble was the first West Point graduate killed during the war. Theodore Winthrop was, according to D.H. Hill, the "only one of the enemy who exhibited an approximation of courage that day."

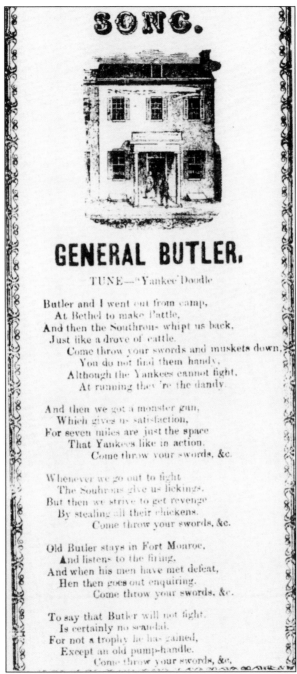

SONG.

GENERAL BUTLER.

TUNE—"Yankee Doodle"

Butler and I went out from camp,
  At Bethel to make battle,
And then the Southrons whipt us back,
  Just like a drove of cattle.
    Come throw your swords and muskets down,
      You do not find them handy,
    Although the Yankees cannot fight,
      At running they're the dandy.

And then we got a monster gun,
  Which gives us satisfaction,
For seven miles are just the space
  That Yankees like in action.
    Come throw your swords, &c.

Whenever we go out to fight
  The Southrons give us lickings,
But then we strive to get revenge
  By stealing all their chickens.
    Come throw your swords, &c.

Old Butler stays in Fort Monroe,
  And listens to the firing,
And when his men have met defeat,
  Hen then goes out enquiring.
    Come throw your swords, &c.

To say that Butler will not fight,
  Is certainly no scandal.
For not a trophy he has gained,
  Except an old pump-handle.
    Come throw your swords, &c.

Big Bethel was a complete failure for the Union. The Federals lost a total of 76 men: 18 killed, 53 wounded, and 5 missing. The Union ineptitude required that a scapegoat be found. Butler was blamed for sending his troops forward with such poor intelligence and for remaining at Fort Monroe during the battle. General Pierce, however, took most of the responsibility for the defeat. He was labeled incompetent and mustered out of the army. The Northern press attempted to salvage some honor and called the Union soldiers courageous as "they fought both friend and foe alike with equal resolution. . . ."

Southerners rejoiced over the Big Bethel victory and laurels were spread everywhere. Confederate casualties were only one killed, seven wounded, and three missing. The dead soldier, Private Henry L. Wyatt of Company B, 1st North Carolina, achieved martyrdom as he had been killed by a shot through the forehead during a volunteer mission to "burn a house between the lines." He was the first Southerner to die in battle and, as Prince John Magruder later wrote, "Too much praise cannot be bestowed upon the heroic soldier who we lost."

It was John Bankhead Magruder, however, who was accorded most of the glory for the Big Bethel victory and was promoted to brigadier general exactly one week following the battle. Southern newspapers called him "the picture of the Virginia gentleman, the frank, manly representative of the chivalry of the dear Old Dominion." Prince John was placed in the Pantheon of Southern Heroes and called "every inch a king." "He's the hero for the times," one ballad proclaimed, "the furious fighting Johnny B. MaGruder."

Four

The Burning
of Hampton

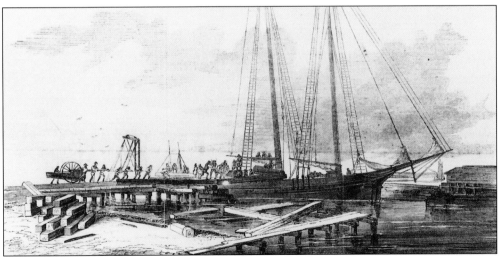

Following the battle of Big Bethel, General Butler appeared content to reinforce his existing positions on the Peninsula. He feared that the Confederates might launch an overwhelming attack. This sketch details how heavy artillery was moved from Fort Monroe to Camp Butler. Butler feared that Newport News Point might be attacked at anytime by the Confederates.

Butler focused on Fort Monroe and strengthened the fort's armaments. On June 14, the massive 12-inch, 52,005-pound "Union" gun arrived. It fired a shell weighing from 360 to 420 pounds. The Union gun was mounted on the carriage that once held the first 15-inch Rodman gun ever built. Both were intended for service against the Confederate batteries at Sewell's Point.

The 15-inch smooth bore cannon dismounted in order to mount the Union gun was originally the largest gun in America. Manufactured by Captain Thomas J. Rodman, the gun weighed 49,100 pounds and was 15 feet 10 inches long. The gun had a range of 5,375 yards and was called the Lincoln Gun.

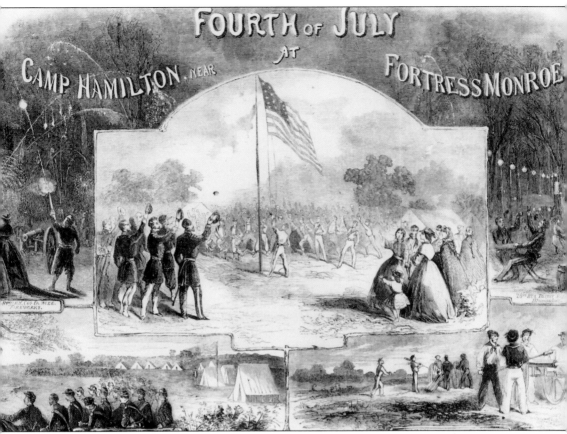

By late June, Butler felt more secure and began to send expeditions into the surrounding countryside. Union troops advanced on June 24 to the vicinity of Big Bethel and plundered nearby farms. Another expedition left Fort Monroe and met two steamers, *Fanny* and *Adriatic*, at the Back River. This force steamed up Harris Creek and destroyed all the vessels they encountered.

This is a view of the 3rd Pennsylvania Heavy Artillery on Fort Monroe's parade ground.

One event that created immediate excitement was the burning of the steamer *Cataline* off the landing at Fort Monroe. The *Cataline* had been used to transport supplies and mail between the fort and Camp Butler on Newport News Point.

General Magruder was distressed by news of Union pillaging and resolved to strike back at the marauding Northerners. Prince John learned that Federal foraging parties regularly marched up the Warwick Road toward Young's Mill. He ordered Lieutenant Colonel William D. Dreux to take troops, including Dreux's Louisiana Battalion, the Wythe Rifles, and some artillery, to ambush the Union excursion. The trap was set near Captain Nelson Smith's home at daybreak on July 5.

The Confederate ambush failed terribly. Dreux and one Louisiana private were killed in this skirmish. Colonel Dreux was the first Louisiana native to be killed in the war and his "death was mourned by all who knew him—on account of his bravery and high military genius."

Magruder, realizing that the Federals frequented the area near Captain Smith's and the Curtis Store along the Warwick Road, planned another trap. He ordered Major John Bell Hood to retaliate. Hood's cavalry struck out at an unsuspecting wood gathering detail of two hundred members of the Hawkins's Zouaves on July 12 at the very spot of Colonel Dreux's death. The surprised Zouaves were routed.

Magruder called the skirmish "a brilliant little affair" and commended John Bell Hood. "Too much praise cannot be bestowed on Major Hood and the cavalry generally for their untiring industry in efforts to meet the enemy," Magruder wrote.

Ben Butler was concerned about his limited knowledge of the Confederate positions and troop strength surrounding the Federal enclave. Thus, Butler secured the services of nationally acclaimed aeronaut John La Mountain. The aeronaut arrived at Fort Monroe on July 23, 1861, equipped with two balloons. His first flight on July 25 was unsuccessful due to high winds; however, on July 31 La Mountain was able to reach an altitude of 1,400 feet and observed a radius of over 30 miles.

La Mountain's observations impressed Butler because he was able to report Confederate troop strength at Sewell's Point and Pig Point. Another ascension on August 1 uncovered that the Confederate camp at Young's Mill housed almost five thousand men and an advance position on Water's Creek was manned by several hundred troops.

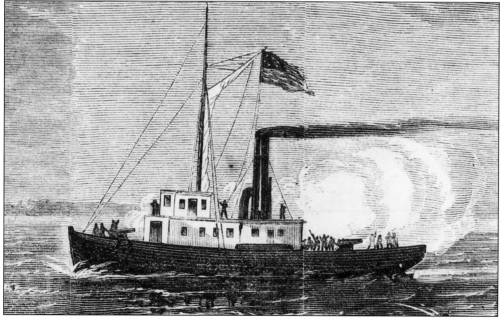

On August 3, 1861, La Mountain made his first flight from the deck of the gunboat *Fanny*. The *Fanny*, with La Mountain's balloon secured to the ship's deck with a windlass and mooring ropes, steamed into the center of Hampton Roads. The balloon reached a height of 2,000 feet and enabled a thorough inspection of Confederate-held Norfolk. A second flight was made on August 10 from the deck of the tug *Adriatic*.

La Mountain had by now used up all of his hydrogen gas-making materials and left Fort Monroe to obtain these supplies. Before he departed, La Mountain proposed to Butler that he could return with a balloon that could "shell, burn or destroy Norfolk." He added, "Ballooning can be made a very useful implement in warfare." Butler agreed, forwarding the concept to the War Department with his endorsement.

The Union position appeared secure on the Peninsula until the Federal army was routed at the 1st Battle of Manassas on July 21, 1861. Winfield Scott ordered Butler to send troops to Washington on July 24 to help defend the Capital. Butler immediately sent the 3rd, 4th, and 5th New York and Baker's California regiment to Washington.

The reduction of four thousand soldiers from the Union command on the Peninsula forced the Federals to abandon Hampton. During their withdrawal a third of the town was burned. Union pickets were simultaneously removed from New Market Creek and repositioned on the Camp Hamilton side of Hampton Creek Bridge.

John Bankhead Magruder decided to take advantage of the Union retrenchment. He organized a strike force and moved against Newport News Point and demanded Camp Butler's surrender on July 28. The strong Union fortifications at Camp Butler discouraged any Confederate attack, and the Federals refused to leave their fortifications to do battle with the Southerners in the open field.

Magruder's attention now shifted to Hampton. On August 6, Prince John, with a force of four thousand infantry, four hundred cavalry, and Randolph's howitzer battalion, moved to within a mile of Hampton. A copy of the *New York Tribune* fell into Magruder's hands, which contained an article stating that Butler intended to use Hampton to house contrabands. Determined not to allow Hampton to be used by Union troops for winter quarters or to become "the harbor of runaway slaves and traitors," and realizing that the Confederates could not hold the town due to its proximity to Fort Monroe, Magruder decided to burn Hampton.

With an agreement from the local soldiers in his command as to the "propriety of this course," and seeing that Butler had already destroyed a third of Hampton when his troops had evacuated the town, Magruder organized a force under the command of Captain Jefferson Curle Phillips of the Old Dominion Dragoons to complete this "loathsome yet patriotic act" prompted by "the foulest desecrations of these houses and homes of our Virginia people by their former Yankee occupants."

Captain Phillips organized a force of five hundred men including the Old Dominion Dragoons, the Mecklenburg Cavalry, the Warwick Beauregards, and the York Rangers. Many of these men owned homes in Hampton. After dark on August 7, Phillips's command moved into Hampton. Phillips sent soldiers throughout the town to warn residents of the impending doom.

Phillips now ordered "that each company would fire one quarter of the town as divided at the cross streets. They went immediately to work. . . . Flames were seen bursting from the buildings on all sides till it appeared that the town was one mass of flames from one end to another."

Sergeant Robert S. Hudgins II of the Old Dominion Dragoons recounted the scene: "As the smoke ascended toward the heavens I was reminded of the ancient sacrifices on the altar to many deities, and I thought of how my little home town was being made a sacrifice to the grim god of war."

"Nothing but a forest of bleak sided chimneys and walls of brick houses tottering and cooling in the wind, scorched and seared trees and heaps of smoldering ruins mark the site," a Union correspondent wrote. "A more desolate sight cannot be imagined than is Hampton today."

Captain Billy Stores, 32nd Virginia Infantry, was one of many local Confederates who participated in the destruction of their home town, and another local soldier, Sergeant Robert S. Hudgins II, recounted the scene of Hampton's burning when he wrote: "At the cross streets it seemed as if hell itself had broken loose, and as if all of its fiery demons were pouring fuel upon the flames. The light of the flames in the sky gave nearly the luster as if it was midday. . . . As we filed out of the town, there rested in the hearts of each of us the realization of a great sacrifice nobly made, and the heroic satisfaction of a soldier's duty well performed."

Even Ben Butler was surprised by the town's burning and thought that "a more wanton and unnecessary act than the burning, as it seems to me, could not have been committed. . . . I confess myself so poor a soldier as not to be able to discern the strategic importance of this

movement. . . . This act upon the part of the enemy seems to me to be a representative one, showing the spirit in which the war is to be carried on on their part, and which perhaps will have a tendency to provoke a corresponding spirit on our part, but we may hope not."

One ironic outcome of the burning of Hampton was the establishment of the Grand Contraband Camp atop Hampton's ruins. The Union forts and camps had become overcrowded with runaway slaves. Hampton, called Slabtown, became the largest contraband camp on the Peninsula. Its existence was the very circumstance that Magruder wished to stop when he ordered the town's destruction.

The Union soldiers were shocked by the Confederate willingness to follow this scorched-earth policy. Lieutenant Charles Brewster wrote: "Such a picture of war and desolation I never saw nor thought of, and hope I shall not again. I pass through the courtyard round the celebrated Hampton Church, the oldest one in use in the United States, it is completely destroyed all but the walls and they are useless."

Five

Ships and Forts

Hampton's burning was the last major offensive move in 1861 on the Peninsula. The Union had been able to maintain its hold on Fort Monroe and Camp Butler. This ensured Federal control of Hampton Roads and a base for operations against Confederate-held territory. This is a photograph of Union officers Lt. Schraft and Dr. John H. Frantz taken while serving at Fort Monroe.

On August 17, 1861, Major General John Ellis Wool replaced Ben Butler as commander of the Union Department of Virginia. The seventy-seven-year-old Wool had served in the U.S. Army for almost fifty years. A hero of the War of 1812, General Wool had achieved his greatest fame during the Mexican War. Wool's actions at the Battle of Buena Vista had earned him the thanks of Congress "for gallant and distinguished conduct."

Major General Wool assumed command and established his headquarters at Fort Monroe's Quarters No. 1. Wool immediately recognized that Fort Monroe's command of Hampton Roads not only limited the Confederate riverine communications between Norfolk and Richmond and blocked these ports' access to the sea, but, more importantly, it provided a valuable springboard for Federal expeditions against other Southern ports.

The first expedition to leave Hampton Roads was on August 26. Commodore Silas H. Stringham's seven-vessel fleet escorted Ben Butler's force enroute to Hatteras Inlet. Hatteras was quickly captured, which assured that the North Carolina Sounds would be under Union control for the rest of the war.

Fort Monroe and Camp Butler quickly became useful staging areas for other major amphibious operations. Flag Officer Samuel F. DuPont launched his Port Royal expedition from Hampton Roads in October 1861. Brigadier General Ambrose E. Burnside's command united with Flag Officer Louis M. Goldsborough's fleet in January 1862 and proceeded to capture Roanoke Island, New Bern, Fort Macon, and Beaufort in North Carolina. Another expedition, Farragut's New Orleans Campaign, left Hampton Roads in February 1862.

General Wool also sought to improve the defensive capabilities of his fortifications. By mid-September both Fort Calhoun and Fort Monroe were well armed with artillery. There were 163 guns and 17 mortars on Fort Monroe alone.

Even though many of Fort Monroe's guns, such as the ninety-six that were mounted in barbette or the thirty-nine mounted in the water battery, were old 32- and 42-pounders, the fort featured other modern weapons. The barbette included two 7-inch rifled guns, eleven 8-inch Columbiads, and ten 10-inch Columbiads. The fort contained a formidable array of firepower which also included a 15-inch Rodman and 12-inch rifled gun positioned near the lighthouse.

At Fort Calhoun, soon to be renamed Fort Wool in honor of Major General John Wool, there were seven 8-inch guns mounted in casemates and two unmounted rifled 42-pounders. The main armament was the 24-pounder Sawyer gun positioned on the fort's wharf aimed at the Confederate Sewell's Point batteries.

Because the Confederates were maintaining pressure all across the quasi-no-man's-land between the Union positions on Hampton Roads and their own fortifications at Young's Mill, Big Bethel, and Howard's Bridge, Wool continued requesting more troops. In October 1861, Wool wrote Washington, "We want more regiments. I only ask that you will give me sufficient number of troops to defend this place. The enemy have been reinforcing their troops."

Since the burning of Hampton, Magruder had kept his primary focus on strengthening his defenses. He constantly entreated Richmond with requests for more troops, artillery, and slaves to work on his series of earthworks he proposed to build across the Peninsula. "I can only hope that Yorktown and Mulberry Island will be made impregnable," Magruder wrote Richmond, "else the Peninsula will be in danger and perhaps Virginia overrun."

Magruder would eventually establish three defensive lines. His forward line of fortifications began at Young's Mill on Deep Creek, crossed the Peninsula to Harwood's Mill and Howard's Bridge on the Poquoson River, and followed that river to Ship's Point on the York River. Magruder's second line began at Mulberry Island on the James River and followed the Warwick River to within one and a half miles of Yorktown. Yorktown was fortified with a series of redoubts, some of which were built atop the British works remaining from the 1781 siege. The fortifications built on Mulberry Island are a prime example of the Confederate defensive preparations. Several trench lines, batteries, and redoubts were built on the island (actually, a peninsula bounded by the Warwick River and Skiffes Creek) which would make Mulberry Island a powerful anchor for the Confederate James River flank. The first defensive work constructed was called Mulberry Island Point Battery. Designed for six cannons, this river battery mounted only four, and Magruder feared that it would be flanked "if the enemy can land at the mouth of the Warwick River." This problem was solved when a covering work was built a half mile away on high ground around the Crafford family farmhouse. Fort Crafford, as it was called, was the largest earthwork in the Warwick line, covering almost 8 acres. The pentagon-shaped fort had an eight-foot-high outer wall, a dry moat, and an inner wall almost 30 feet high. Magruder called Fort Crafford, armed with eight heavy cannons and with emplacements for eight smaller pieces, "very strong" and considered the fort capable of withstanding a month-long siege.

Even though the works around Yorktown were very extensive, as visible in this photograph by George H. Houghton, a third defensive line was constructed outside of Williamsburg. This line, first proposed by Colonel Benjamin S. Ewell, comprised a series of fourteen redoubts, complete with supporting redans and rifle pits, between College and Queen's Creeks, with its center anchored by Fort Magruder (Redoubt #6) astride the Williamsburg Road.

The Confederate Gloucester Point fortifications pictured here are typical of the tremendous effort made by the soldiers defending the Peninsula to secure their army's position. By late winter 1862, both commanders on the Peninsula were still concerned, however, that the enemy could overrun their positions, thereby jeopardizing their nation. Magruder and Wool recognized the Peninsula's strategic importance: as a springboard for attack and as an avenue of defense. Beginning in March 1862, the eyes of America would focus on the Peninsula for these very reasons.

Six

Ironclads

Hampton Roads was the scene of one of history's greatest naval engagements, the March 9, 1862, first battle between ironclads. This duel between the U.S.S. *Monitor* and C.S.S. *Virginia* (*Merrimack*) changed naval warfare forever. No longer would wooden sailing ships rule the waves, for iron vessels became the key to naval superiority.

When Virginia left the Union, local volunteers were able to quickly secure the Gosport Navy Yard in Portsmouth. The yard's capture was a virtual godsend for the ship-poor Confederacy. Gosport had been the U.S. Navy's largest navy yard, and its evacuation was bungled by the yard's commander Commodore C.S. McCauley. An effort was made to destroy the yard and save various ships before the Confederates could seize it, but the job was badly done. The dry dock was not destroyed, foundries were unharmed, and over one thousand cannons were left behind.

Perhaps one of the most important items left behind during the yard's destruction and evacuation was the U.S.S. *Merrimack*. Commissioned in 1856, the *Merrimack* was considered "a magnificent specimen of naval architecture." The vessel had one major defect: its engines were unsatisfactory and the *Merrimack* operated more often on sail power. The *Merrimack* was sent to Norfolk for repairs on February 16, 1860, and she remained there until the secession crisis reached Virginia.

The U.S. Navy endeavored to remove the *Merrimack* from the Gosport Navy Yard on April 20, but failed and the ship was scuttled by the retreating Federals. The Confederates immediately occupied the yard and raised the damaged frigate. Confederate Secretary of the Navy Stephen R. Mallory decided to transform the damaged *Merrimack* into an ironclad. Mallory believed that "the possession of an iron-armored ship as a matter of the first necessity. Such a vessel at this time could traverse the entire coast of the United States, prevent all blockades, and encounter, with a fair prospect of success, their entire Navy. . . . unequality of numbers may be compensated by invulnerability; and thus not only does economy but naval success dictate the wisdom and expediency of fighting with iron against wood. . . ." He selected Lieutenant John Mercer Brooke and Naval Constructor John L. Porter to complete the conversion. The *Merrimack's* transformation into an ironclad was a remarkable test of Confederate ingenuity.

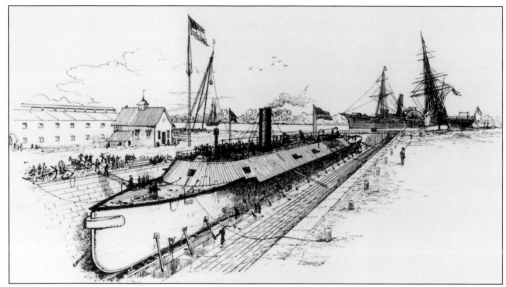

The *Merrimack* was totally reconfigured during its conversion. An 178-foot-long casemate, covered by 4 inches of ironplate bolted to 24 inches of oak and pine backing, was constructed atop the ship's hull. The ironclad was armed with six 9-inch Dahlgren smoothbores, two 6.4-inch Brooke rifles, and two 7-inch Brooke rifles which served as pivot guns. A 6-foot-long, 1,500-pound cast-iron ram, bolted 2 feet under water, completed the vessel's weaponry.

The *Merrimack* was launched on February 17, 1862, and recommissioned as the C.S.S. *Virginia*. The *Virginia* appeared to be a powerful vessel, but there were several defects. The ram was poorly mounted and the hull was only armored with 1 inch of ironplate. With her 268-foot length and draught of 22 feet, the *Virginia* proved to be difficult to maneuver. The two salvaged 600-horsepower engines of the old *Merrimack* were reused to propel the *Virginia*. Lieutenant John Taylor Wood noted that the ironclad "was as unmanageable as a waterlogged vessel."

Flag Officer Franklin Buchanan was selected by Secretary Mallory to command the new ironclad. Buchanan was an excellent choice. A Marylander and grandson of a signer of the Declaration of Independence, he had been in the U.S. Navy since 1815. Franklin Buchanan had served as the first superintendent of the United States Naval Academy at Annapolis and was in command of the Washington Naval Yard when the war broke out. He resigned his commission following the April 19, 1861 Baltimore riots. As soon as Buchanan assumed command of the C.S.S. *Virginia* on February 24, 1862, he readied the ironclad for combat.

The U.S. Navy was well aware of the Confederate ironclad project and believed that it had an adequate force in Hampton Roads to defeat the *Virginia*. The fleet included the U.S.S. *Roanoke*, U.S.S. *St. Lawrence*, U.S.S. *Minnesota*, the U.S.S. *Congress*, and the U.S.S. *Cumberland* (pictured here) as well as various support vessels.

Franklin Buchanan decided that his first attack should be made against the two Union sailing vessels stationed off Newport News Point, the 50-gun U.S.S. *Congress* and the 24-gun U.S.S. *Cumberland*. The *Cumberland* was his primary target, as Buchanan understood that she was armed with a powerful 70-pounder rifle, the only weapon he thought capable of damaging his ironclad.

On March 8, 1862, the C.S.S. *Virginia* steamed out of the Elizabeth River and crossed Hampton Roads toward Newport News Point. The entire Union fleet went to battle stations with the shout "that thing is a-comin at last sir." The *Virginia* appeared like "the roof of a very big barn belching forth smoke as from a chimney on fire." It took the *Virginia* over an hour to reach Newport News Point. Once there, the Confederate ironclad by-passed the U.S.S. *Congress* and the Union batteries at Camp Butler and headed straight for the U.S.S. *Cumberland*.

As the *Virginia* began her run at the *Cumberland*, the Union ships and shore batteries began shelling the ironclad with little impact. The shot "had no effect on her," noted Lieutenant Thomas O. Selfridge, "but glanced off like pebble stones." The Confederate ironclad then rammed the *Cumberland*'s starboard side, creating a hole, according to Lieutenant John Taylor Wood, "wide enough to drive in a horse and cart." "The noise of the crashing timbers was heard above the din of battle," noted Catesby Jones. The Confederates were jubilant as Lieutenant Robert Minor exclaimed, "We've sunk the *Cumberland*." Minor would later write that the "crash into the *Cumberland* was terrific in its results. Our cleaver fairly opened her side." The *Cumberland* was mortally wounded, the ramming made only worse by a shot from the *Virginia*'s bow rifle which killed ten men. The Union ship immediately began to sink and trapped the *Virginia*'s ram within her. The *Virginia*'s engines struggled to free her from being pulled under the waves with the *Cumberland*. The ironclad survived only because her ram broke off.

The *Virginia* backed away and continued to pour shot and shell into the *Cumberland*. The Union vessel refused to surrender. Finally, the *Cumberland* lurched forward and sank with all her flags flying as Executive Officer (and acting commander) Lieutenant George U. Morris called to his crew, "Give them a Broadside boys, as she goes."

Buchanan now turned his ironclad toward the *Congress*. The Union ship had run aground trying to escape, and the *Virginia* could only approach within a hundred yards, yet pounded the *Congress* with shot and shell for almost an hour until the *Congress* surrendered.

Buchanan ordered two of his support vessels, the C.S.S. *Raleigh* and the C.S.S. *Beaufort*, to finalize the surrender. However, Brigadier General John Mansfield ordered his men and batteries at Camp Butler to open fire on the Confederates. Buchanan was enraged and while standing on top of the *Virginia* to gain a better view of the action, he was seriously wounded when a Union minie ball entered his thigh.

Franklin Buchanan was carried below and ordered his executive officer, Lieutenant Catesby ap Roger Jones, to "Plug hot shot into her and don't leave until she's afire." Jones assumed command of the *Virginia* and soon the *Congress* was totally ablaze. "Dearly did they pay," wrote Lieutenant John R. Eggleston, "for their unparalleled treachery."

The Federal fleet had tried to respond to the emergence of the Confederate ironclad. The *Minnesota* (pictured here), *Roanoke*, and *St. Lawrence* had all run aground moving from Newport News Point. Jones now moved the *Virginia* toward the *Minnesota*, but could only approach to within a mile of the Union vessel because the tide had ebbed. As darkness began to shroud Hampton Roads, the *Virginia* returned to Sewell's Point determined to destroy the rest of the Northern fleet on the next day.

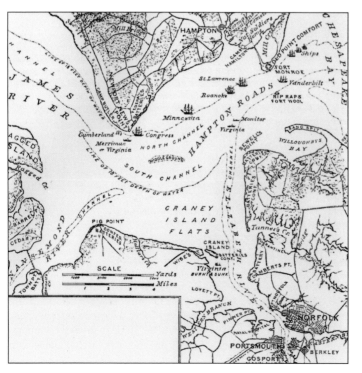

Abraham Lincoln viewed the March 8 events as the greatest Union calamity since Bull Run. Secretary of War Edwin W. Stanton feared that the *Merrimack* would soon "come up the Potomac and disperse Congress, destroy the Capitol and public buildings." Little did the Northern leaders realize that the Confederate ironclad was considered by its commander so unseaworthy that it could not leave Hampton Roads.

As the Union leaders feared for the worse, a virtual miracle was taking place. The U.S.S. *Monitor* entered in Hampton Roads aglow from the flames consuming the *Congress*. The Union ironclad positioned itself next to the U.S.S. *Minnesota* to await the return of the C.S.S. *Virginia* in the morning.

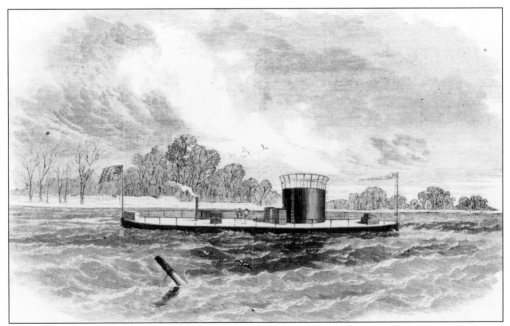

The U.S.S. *Monitor* was a completely new concept of naval design created by Swedish inventor John Ericsson. It was an engineering marvel, containing several patents created by Ericsson for his ship. The *Monitor* was 173 feet in length, weighed 776 tons, and had a beam of 41.5 feet. The ironclad's draft was 11 feet with a freeboard of less than 1 foot. It was virtually awash with the sea. All of the ship's machinery, magazine, and quarters were positioned below the waterline. The turret and pilothouse were the only features protruding from the deck.

The *Monitor*'s most impressive feature
was its steam-powered, rotating, circular
turret mounting two 11-inch Dahlgrens.
The turret was constructed of eight
layers of 1-inch-thick, curved, rolled
plates. The gun ports were equipped
with shutters. The turret had an interior
diameter of 20 feet and a height of
9 feet.

Lieutenant John Lorimer Worden
was selected as the *Monitor*'s
commander. Worden had served in
the U.S. Navy since 1834 and had
been a prisoner of the Confederates
after conducting a secret mission to
Fort Pickens, in Pensacola Bay, Florida.
Recently exchanged, Worden accepted
the command and commented, "After
a hasty examination of her," he
was, "induced to believe that she may
prove a success. At all events, I am
quite willing to be an agent in testing
her capabilities."

The *Monitor* was commissioned on February 25, 1862. Lieutenant Worden assembled a hand-picked crew, which would eventually number sixteen officers and forty-nine men. This photograph shows the ironclad's officers, as follows, from left to right: (top row) Albert B. Campbell (2nd assistant engineer), Mark Trueman Sunstrom (3rd assistant engineer), William F. Keeler (acting assistant paymaster), and L. Howard Newman (lieutenant, executive officer of the U.S.S. *Galena*); (middle row) Louis N. Stodder (acting master), George Frederickson (master's mate), William Flye (acting volunteer lieutenant), Daniel C. Longue (acting assistant surgeon), and Samuel Dana Greene (lieutenant); (bottom row) Robinson W. Hands (3rd assistant engineer) and E..V. Gager (acting master).

On the afternoon of March 6, 1862, the U.S.S. *Monitor* left New York under tow by the steam tug *Seth Low*, accompanied by the steamers *Sachem* and *Camtuck*. The *Monitor* encountered severe storms off the New Jersey coast and almost sank enroute to Hampton Roads. Somehow the *Monitor* survived the angry sea. Lieutenant S. Dana Greene later wrote about the stormy trip from New York: "I think I lived 10 good years."

Catesby Jones got the *Virginia* underway from its mooring early in the morning on March 9 accompanied by the steamers *Patrick Henry, Jamestown,* and *Teazer.* A heavy fog delayed the small fleet's entrance into Hampton Roads until nearly 8:00 am. Jones saw that the *Minnesota* was still aground, and the *Virginia* headed straight for the Union frigate. The *Monitor* now moved out away from the *Minnesota.* The Confederates were amazed by this sight. Lieutenant James H. Rochelle of the *Patrick Henry* noted, "Such a craft as the eyes of a seaman never looked upon before—an immense shingle floating in the water, with a gigantic cheesebox rising from its center; no sails, no wheels, no smokestack, no guns. What could it be?" Jones instantly recognized it as Ericsson's iron battery.

The *Monitor* headed straight for the *Virginia* and continued to block the *Virginia's* path toward the *Minnesota.* Worden knew that his ironclad was the only thing that could save the *Minnesota.* The *Minnesota's* captain had made it very clear that he intended to destroy his grounded ship if threatened by the *Virginia.*

The *Monitor* opened fire at 8:45 am and for the next four hours the two ironclads pounded each other mercilessly with shot and shell. The battle was mostly fought at a range of less than 100 yards.

Worden hoped that by firing his heavy shot, 168-pound spherical projectiles using 15 pounds of powder, from the *Monitor*'s 11-inch Dahlgrens, such pounding would loosen or break the *Virginia*'s ironplates. In turn, the *Virginia* was at a disadvantage. She had only explosive shells, hot shot, and canister specifically to use against wooden vessels. Thus, Jones's strategy was first to concentrate on the *Minnesota* and if necessary to try to ram or board the *Monitor*.

The *Monitor*'s small size and quickness frustrated the Southerners, who tried to fire at the *Monitor*'s gun ports but discovered that the turret revolved too quickly. The *Monitor*'s turret truly amazed the Confederates, yet the Federal shot continued to bounce off the sloped, iron sides of the *Virginia*.

There were several problems on board the *Monitor* despite her many technological advantages. The port stoppers proved to be almost too heavy to operate and only one gun could be fired at a time. Both ports were left open because it was the only way to enhance the gun crew's vision since the communication system between the pilothouse and turret failed to perform. The turret's rotating system also malfunctioned due to water damage which caused the mechanism to rust. Thus, the turret could not be stopped with any precision. Eventually, the guns were discharged "on the fly" as the turret turned past the target.

After almost two hours of combat, Worden took the *Monitor* out of action to replenish ammunition in the turret. Jones took immediate advantage and moved the *Virginia* toward the *Minnesota*. The Confederate ironclad, leaking from the loss of her ram, ran aground. The *Virginia*, unable to deflect its guns to defend itself, was pounded by the *Monitor*. "Our situation was critical," wrote Chief Engineer Ashton Ramsay. "The *Monitor* could, at her leisure, come up close to us. . . . In she came and began to sound every chink in our armor—everyone but that which was actually vulnerable, had she known it. The coal consumption of the two day's fight had lightened our prow until our unprotected submerged deck was almost awash. The armor on our sides below the waterline had been extended but about three feet, owing to our hasty departure before the work was finished. Lightened as we were, these exposed portions rendered us no longer an ironclad, and the *Monitor* might have pierced us between wind and water had she depressed her guns. Fearing that she might discover our vulnerable 'heel of Achilles,' we had to take all chances. We lashed down the safety valves, heaped quick burning combustibles into the already raging fires, and brought the boilers to a pressure that would have been unsafe under ordinary circumstances." Somehow, the old engines responded to the need and the *Virginia* freed herself. Jones then tried to ram the *Monitor*. The Union ironclad was hit with a glancing blow which caused no damage to the *Monitor*, but instead injured the *Virginia*. The impact caused another leak in the *Virginia's* bow.

The *Monitor*'s evasive action enabled Jones to once again maneuver toward the *Minnesota*. Several shots were sent against the stranded frigate, one of which struck the tug *Dragon*. The *Dragon*'s boiler burst and the tug, which had been alongside the *Minnesota* to tow that vessel to safety, sank. This image is a tintype of one of the *Virginia*'s gunnery officers, Lieutenant John Pembroke Jones.

Worden was able to steer his ship between the Confederate ironclad and the Union frigate. He now decided to ram the *Virginia*, seeking to strike the larger ironclad's propeller to disable her. The *Monitor* missed her target because of a malfunctioning steering system.

As the Union ship passed the stern of the *Virginia*, Lieutenant John Taylor Wood (pictured here) fired his 7-inch Brooke pivot gun at the *Monitor*'s pilothouse. The shell struck the observation slit as Worden was peering out. The explosion created "a flash of light and a cloud of smoke which blinded Worden."

The *Monitor*, with no one at the helm, veered off onto the shoal. Worden was taken below for treatment. The *Monitor* appeared out of action as minutes ticked by while Executive Officer Dana Greene made his way from the turret to the pilothouse. Jones considered renewing the attack against the *Minnesota*, but the receding tide prompted him to take his ironclad back to Sewell's Point. Greene had finally taken over command as the *Virginia* steamed away, but he did not pursue the Confederate vessel.

A Union soldier, Asher Williams, summed up the dramatic events when he wrote from Camp Butler: "We had a lively time here three weeks ago. The rebel steamer *Merrimac* with five other gunboats attacked this place. They succeeded in destroying two men of war stationed here and then commenced shelling the camp, nearly all their shells went over the camp doing up no damage. They left us to seek another of our vessels, but concluded to wait until morning as the *Minnesota* (our vessel) had run aground. Next morning, the *Merrimac* was seen steaming towards the *Minnesota* to annihilate her as she had done the others but how woefully they were mistaken for during the night a box of iron called the *Monitor* had arrived and gave the rebels more than they bargained for after five hours the rebels gave it up. We are momentarily expecting her again. . . . They will find us ready as soon as they get ready." Secretary Mallory wanted the *Virginia* to attack New York City, writing Franklin Buchanan that the Confederate ironclad "could shell and burn the city and shipping. Such an event would eclipse all the glories of the combat of the sea . . . and would strike a blow from which the enemy could never recover." Buchanan replied that the "*Virginia* is yet an experiment, and by no means invulnerable as has already been proved in her conflict on the 8 and 9. . . . The *Virginia* may probably succeed in passing Old Point Comfort and the Rip Raps [but] . . . she has yet to be tested in a seaway. . . . Should she encounter a gale, or a very heavy swell, I think it is more probable she would founder." Buchanan concluded that "the *Virginia* [is] the most important protection to the safety of Norfolk. . . ."

Neither ship had been seriously damaged during the four-hour battle and both claimed victory. The *Monitor* had indeed won a tactical victory, as the Union ironclad had stopped the *Virginia* from destroying the *Minnesota*. However, the strategic victor was the *Virginia* because its mere existence enabled the Confederates to control Hampton Roads and the entrance to the James River, thereby defending the water approach to Norfolk and Richmond.

The Federals feared that the *Virginia* would try to steam out of Hampton Roads and recognized that the *Monitor* was the only weapon in her path. Lieutenant William N. Jeffers assumed command of the *Monitor* after the March 9 battle and was ordered that "the *Monitor* be not too much exposed, and that in no event shall any attempt be made to proceed with her unattended to Norfolk."

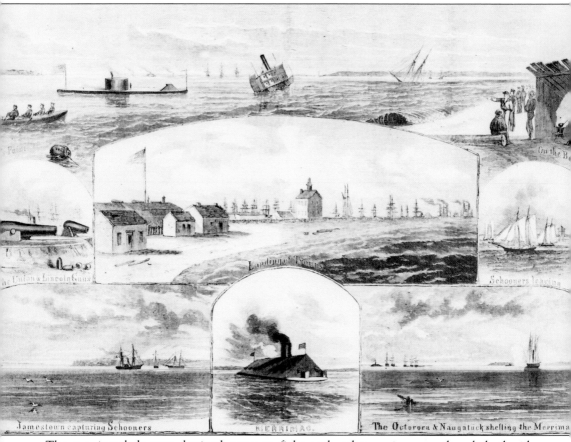

The two ironclads were destined never to fight each other again, even though both sides concocted schemes for capturing their enemy's vessels. The *Virginia* appeared in Hampton Roads again on April 11, having been repaired and fitted with a new ram. Her commander was the former U.S. Navy forty-eight-year veteran and hero Flag Officer Josiah N. Tattnal. Tattnal hoped to draw the *Monitor* up into Hampton Roads to use his gunboats to board and capture the Union vessel. In turn, the Federal navy had created its own plan of tempting the *Virginia* into the Chesapeake Bay, where the Confederate ironclad could be rammed and captured. Although a show of force was repeated several times during the following weeks, neither ship was willing to commit itself to battle.

Seven

The Peninsula Campaign

Major General George Brinton McClellan had assumed command of the Army of the Potomac following the Union debacle at Bull Run. "Little Mac," as he was fondly known, transformed the defeated and disorganized army into a magnificent military machine. Yet, he hesitated to use it in battle.

Goaded by Lincoln to develop some plan of action against the Confederate capital, McClellan eventually decided to strike at Richmond by way of the Virginia Peninsula. It was a sound concept. A direct approach through Northern Virginia could be costly in casualties, while a move between the James and York Rivers could utilize Union naval superiority: gunboats could protect his flanks and river steamers could carry his troops. The C.S.S. *Virginia* had changed the strategic balance in Hampton Roads and closed the James River to the Federal fleet. McClellan, confident that the *Monitor* could hold the Confederate ironclad at bay, decided to proceed with his campaign.

During March 1862, 389 vessels would deliver to Fort Monroe and Camp Butler 121,500 men, 14,592 animals, 1,224 vehicles, 44 artillery batteries, 103 siege guns, "and the enormous quantity of equipage . . . required for an army of such magnitude." The Army of the Potomac was the largest army and amphibious operation previously witnessed in North America.

George McClellan arrived on the Peninsula on April 2, 1862, happy to be free of "that sink of inequity" in Washington. His demotion from commander-in-chief of the U.S. Army to commander of just the Army of the Potomac made him now determined to achieve success. Despite the advice of his chief engineer, John G. Barnard, to move against Norfolk first, McClellan decided to march against Yorktown and Gloucester Point and then establish his base at West Point for his attack on Richmond.

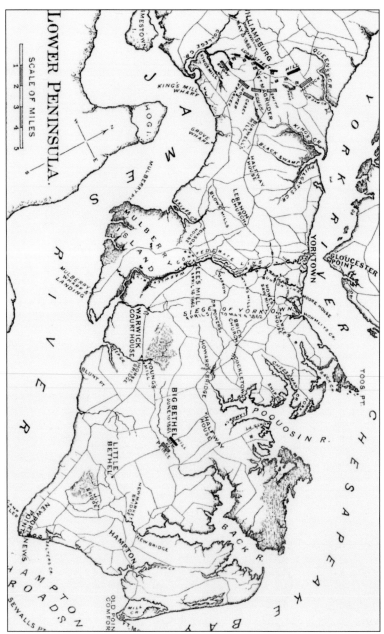

Since the James River was declared by the Union navy closed to the operations of their vessels by the combined influence of the enemy's batteries on its banks and the Confederate fleet, McClellan resolved to flank the Confederates out of their positions at Yorktown, thereby opening the James River with a Southern retreat. McClellan's information, provided by the detective Allan Pinkerton and Major General John E. Wool, indicated that Magruder's 15,000-strong force was at Yorktown, with his right flank unsecured. The Federal commander thought he could interpose his troops across the Confederate line of retreat, trapping Prince John at Yorktown like General George Washington had cornered Lord Cornwallis. Maps provided by General Wool indicated good roads and no water barriers, so McClellan seemed confident of a quick victory on the lower Peninsula.

Brigadier General Samuel P. Heintzelman's III Corps, followed by elements of Brigadier General Edwin Vose Sumner's II Corps, was to march on the Hampton-York Road through Big Bethel directly to Yorktown so to hold Magruder in his defenses. McClellan believed that Heintzelman's advance would flank the Confederates out of their Young's Mill strong point. The path would then be clear for Brigadier General Erasmus Darwin Keyes's IV Corps to march up the Warwick Road to the Half-Way House northwest of Yorktown, thereby cutting the Confederate line of retreat.

The Union army began its march on April 4, 1862. Keyes's IV Corps marched up the Warwick Road with Brigadier General W.F. "Baldy" Smith's division, supported by the 5th U.S. Cavalry, in the advance. The Federals brushed aside Confederate pickets at Water's Creek and prepared to encounter the Southern "strong works and . . . force at Young's Mill." When Smith's division reached the mill, Keyes (pictured here) reported, "the enemy retreated at our approach firing only a few shots." The IV Corps had reached its goal for the first day's march without any bloodshed.

Keyes's troops were amazed at the extensive Confederate works at Young's Mill as Private Wilbur Fisk of the 2nd Vermont recalled that "We drove the enemy from a position they had fortified and that night occupied the place ourselves. The rebels left quite a village of huts or barracks, and from appearances, they had enjoyed much more comfortable quarters during the winter than we had ourselves." Keyes reported to McClellan that "The enemy's works at Young's Mill are so strong that with 5,000 men he might have stopped by two divisions there a week. . . ."

The IV Corps began its march at 6 am on April 5. Smith's division once again led the march. Soon it began to rain, "pouring in torrents, rendering the roads-nigh impassable," which slowed the troops' progress.

Then, around 11 am, the march was stopped by the Confederates occupying a strong position at the Lee's Mill crossing of the Warwick River. Neither Lee's Mill, the Warwick River's course across the Peninsula, nor the Confederate fortifications were noted on the maps available to the Union command.

The Federals were shocked by the "very serious resistance they encountered at Lee's Mill." "Flames appeared on all sides," reported Baldy Smith as his men approached the river, and he was forced to advise Keyes that "we shall not be able to reach the Half-Way House on the Yorktown-Williamsburg Road today. . . ."

The crossing at Lee's Mill was held by approximately eighteen hundred Confederates under the overall command of Brigadier General Lafayette McLaws (pictured here). Lee's Mill was considered a "naturally strong position" by Magruder's Chief of Artillery Colonel H.C. Cabell. All the approaches to this mill dam crossing were covered by redoubts constructed along the mill pond or overlooking the Warwick as it "follows a tortuous course through salt marshes . . . from which the land rises up boldly to a height of 30 or 40 feet."

General Keyes wrote McClellan that "Magruder is in a strongly fortified position behind the Warwick Road, the fords to which have been destroyed by dams, and the approaches to which are through dense forests, swamps, and marshes. No part of this line as discovered can be taken without an enormous waste of life." Federal Chief Engineer Brigadier General John G. Barnard concurred with Keyes's assessment and remarked that "the line is certainly one of the most extensive known to modern times."

The brief engagement at Lee's Mill cost the Confederates ten casualties, but it had far-reaching implications. His advance blocked by the unexpected array of enemy entrenchment, McClellan resolved to deploy the 103 siege guns he had brought to the Peninsula and lay siege to Magruder's defenses.

McClellan's hesitation at the Warwick River set the stage for a carefully organized Confederate ruse. Magruder began shuttling his soldiers, such as Private Andrew Skidmore (pictured here in his pre-war militia uniform), to create an illusion of many troops arriving on his line and moving into positions of great strength. Private Edmund Dewitt Patterson of the 4th Alabama wrote that he and his fellow Confederate soldiers "have been travelling most of the day . . . with no other view than to show ourselves to the enemy, at as many different points of the line as possible."

Magruder earned the title of the "Master of Ruses and Strategy" for this make-believe show of strength. "It was a wonderful thing," recorded diarist Mary Chesnut, "how he played his ten thousand before McClellan like fireflies and utterly deluded him. . . ." Prince John once again became a leading hero of the Southland. "The assuming and maintaining of the line by Magruder, with his small force in face of such overwhelming odds," wrote Brigadier General Jubal A. Early, "was one of the boldest exploits ever performed by a military commander. . . ."

Magruder was surprised that his thirteen thousand men could create such an impression, as he wrote Richmond that McClellan "to my utter surprise . . . permitted day after day to elapse without an assault. In a few days the object of his delay was apparent. In every direction; in front of our lines; the intervening woods, and along the open fields, earthworks began to appear. . . ."

Once his engineers conducted their surveys of the Confederate defenses, McClellan decided to concentrate his siege engineering on Yorktown. His plan was to assault the Confederate works in the vicinity of the historic town once his heavy artillery had breached them. "Little Mac" laid out fifteen batteries for the heavy 8- and 13- inch seacoast mortars and enormous 100- and 200-pound Parrott guns as well as 20- and 30-pound Parrott and 4.5 inch Rodman siege rifles he had brought to the Peninsula.

McClellan's men were put to work, under intermittent fire from the Confederate lines, building the roads, rifle pits, and gun emplacements necessary to eventually pound the Confederates into submission. Thomas B. Leaver of New Hampshire wrote that "It seems the fight has to be won partially through the implements of peace, the shovel, axe and pick."

As the Union soldiers dug and piled sandbags on parapets, the Confederates continued their demonstrations. The Southerners at Dam No.1 would often cross the river at night to establish picket posts on the Federal side of the dam. Confederate W.H. Andrews remembered wading through the cold water along the dam on the evening of April 15 and reaching close enough to the Union pickets "to hear them whisper."

Many Union officers believed the Confederate line could be broken at several weak points along the Warwick River. Since the siege's first day, Baldy Smith had wanted to attack the Confederate line, but McClellan had rejected the thought of any such move, telegraphing President Lincoln on April 7: "The Warwick River grows worse the more you look at it."

On April 15, 1862, General McClellan reviewed Smith's position at Garrow's Field across from Dam No. 1. The place had been named by the Vermont troops holding the position as Burnt Chimneys for the three stark chimneys that defined the site as the only remaining remnant of the Garrow family farm. The house, Merry Oaks, had been burned by the Confederates in what appeared to be, according to Confederate artillerist Henry Berkley, as "a useless . . . destruction of private property . . . but such is war."

McClellan, having observed the continued Confederate defensive preparations, approved an infantry attack to gain control of Dam No. 1. On the morning of April 16, Baldy Smith deployed Brigadier General W.T.H. Brooks's (pictured here) Vermont Brigade along the river. As the 3rd and 4th Vermont deployed as skirmishers, Captain Thaddeus P. Mott's 3rd New York Battery began shelling the Confederate works across the Warwick River.

Baldy Smith reinforced his position with Captain Romeryn B. Ayres's Battery F, 5th U.S. Artillery and Captain Charles C. Wheeler's Battery E, 1st New York Artillery. After three hours of cannon and rifle fire, the Southerners appeared to have abandoned their one-gun battery defending the dam. General Smith made a personal reconnaissance of the Confederate positions and reported, "that the gun in the angle of the upper work had been replaced by a wooden gun, and that scarcely anybody showed above the parapet." The Federals now realized that the Confederate position at Dam No.1 was extremely weak and could perhaps be carried with an assault.

Baldy Smith sent four companies of the 3rd Vermont across the river to capture the Confederate rife pits below the dam. If the Vermonters were successful in driving the enemy out of their rifle pits, they were to cheer and wave a white handkerchief and more troops would be sent across the Warwick. Captain Alonzo Hutchinson (pictured here) was entrusted with General Brooks's handkerchief with which to make the signal for reinforcements.

The Vermonters, 192 hand-picked men, crossed the Warwick under heavy fire and captured the enemy's position along the water's edge. It had been a difficult passage. The Vermonters had to carry their muskets and cartridge boxes over their heads while contending with a muddy, root-filled river bottom and trees felled by the Confederates to serve as obstacles.

The Confederate unit holding the rifle pits, the 15th North Carolina, had been surprised by the Vermonter's bold rush and fell back in panic that one Vermonter, Erastus Buck, thought made them "look like a flock of sheep." It was the North Carolinians' first day in the trenches and their first battle. The 15th's commander, Lieutenant Colonel William McKinney, tried to rally and reform his men, but he was killed instantly by a ball through the forehead. The 15th then huddled behind a redoubt and the entire Confederate line at Dam No. 1 was in disarray. Pictured here is Private Stanley M. Riggsbee of the 15th North Carolina.

The Green Mountain Boys, however, were also in a dangerous position. Most of their ammunition was wet and useless. Expected reinforcements never materialized. Captain Hutchinson lay mortally wounded on the banks of the Warwick, unable to give the signal for reinforcements. It would not have mattered if he did because Baldy Smith had taken his second fall from his horse and was somewhat senseless.

Leadership among the Vermonters across the Warwick had fallen on the shoulders of Captain Samuel E. Pingree. Pingree, however, was seriously wounded—his thumb shot off in addition to his bleeding profusely from a wound to the hip. Meanwhile, the Confederate lines were stirring like a hornet's nest.

Brigadier General Howell Cobb, a former governor of Georgia and commander of Cobb's Legion, reinforced the 15th North Carolina. Cobb reorganized the Confederate troops, "riding in among the men," according to Lafayette McLaws, and "they recognized his voice and his person, and promptly retook their positions." The Vermonters, under heavy pressure from the Confederate counterattack, reluctantly withdrew across the Warwick. Regaining their rifle pits, the resurgent Rebels continued their fire and made the water "boil with their bullets." The Union troops suffered a majority of their casualties while recrossing the "fatal stream."

Baldy Smith, apparently now lucid, decided to try the Confederate lines again. Late in the afternoon, following a Federal cannonade from twenty-two guns, Smith sent units from Colonel Edwin Stoughton's (pictured here) 4th Vermont to cross above the dam and troops from Colonel Lord's 6th Vermont to cross below the dam to break the Confederate line. The attack was unsuccessful. By dark, the Battle of Dam No. 1 was over, with 165 Federal and 145 Confederate casualties.

General W.F. "Baldy" Smith reflected after the battle that among the men of the 3rd Vermont who crossed the river, there were "more individual acts of heroism performed than he had ever heard of." The Confederates even referred to the Vermonters as "brave rascals." Two Medals of Honor would be awarded for gallantry on April 16. Captain Samuel E. Pingree, later governor of Vermont, received his in 1891 for bravery during the engagement. The other was presented to musician Julian Scott (pictured here) in February 1865. The sixteen-year-old Scott crossed the river at least two times following the first assault saving "no less than nine of his comrades."

One of the men Julian Scott attempted to save was mortally wounded Private William Scott. Scott was known as the sleeping sentinel and had been pardoned by Abraham Lincoln in late 1861 from a firing squad. His reprieve had led him to say, "I will show President Lincoln that I am not afraid to die for my country." Scott fulfilled his pledge at Dam No. 1.

The battle was the Vermont Brigade's first engagement, and General McClellan called the Vermonters' conduct "worthy of veterans." Corporal George Q. French wrote his friends at home about the battle: "The 3rd Vermont has won a name, but Oh! at what a cost." Despite the heroism, many Union soldiers called the battle nothing but a "Dam failure." General Smith merely concluded, "Thus a fair opportunity to break the Warwick line was missed. . . ."

General Joseph E. Johnston assumed command on the Peninsula the day after the Battle of Dam No. 1. Soon the entire Confederate army was manning the trenches between Yorktown and Mulberry Island. Even though Johnston lauded Magruder's "delaying tactics," he believed that the Confederates should abandon the Peninsula. He wrote Jefferson Davis that "No one but McClellan could have hesitated to attack. The fight for Yorktown must be one of artillery, in which we cannot win. The result is certain; the time only doubtful."

The siege was to last another two weeks. McClellan concentrated on building emplacements for his heavy guns and parallel trenches in preparation for the bombardment which would force the Confederate evacuation of the Warwick-Yorktown Line. Brigadier General Fitz-John Porter coordinated the construction of the Union siege lines facing Yorktown.

The siege's monotony was occasionally broken by the sight of balloons floating over the lines. Professor T.S.C. Lowe's two gas balloons, *Intrepid* and *Constitution*, were launched almost daily during the siege. The Confederates responded with their own crude hot-air balloon and the first anti-aircraft guns as Major E.P. Alexander elevated his artillery to send shot and shell against Union aerial observers.

"It was worth a man's life to show his head above the works," wrote Sergeant W.H. Andrews of the 1st Georgia Regulars about the constant rifle and cannon fire. The Union deployed companies from Colonel Hiram Berdan's (pictured here) Sharpshooters at various locations up and down the 12-mile line. Either hidden in rifle pits or concealed in treetop positions, the sharpshooters added a fierceness to the siege and were "as audacious and deadly." Confederate artillerist Robert Stiles considered them "a fearful thing. The regular sharpshooter often seems to me little better than a human tiger lying in wait for blood."

ANOTHER GENERAL-IN-CHIEF
McCLELLAN, WITH HIS WIFE

The siege dragged on, and with it the soldiers suffered from exposure and poor food. Lieutenant Robert H. Miller of the Concordia Rifles wrote his mother from Wynne's Mill that he and his men "have dug Rifle pits and are compelled to eat-sleep and stand-in from day to night and from night to day." It rained almost daily, adding to the misery as the soldiers had to stand in trenches "with water up to our knees," wrote Sergeant W.H. Andrews.

McClellan planned to unleash his grand bombardment on the Confederate lines on May 5 and advised President Lincoln, "I see the way clear to success and hope to make it brilliant, although with but little loss of life." But the siege was not to end as McClellan expected. On May 3, the Confederates unleashed a tremendous bombardment to cover their retreat toward Williamsburg. By morning, their trenches were empty.

Eight

The Battle
of Williamsburg

As McClellan made his final preparations for his grand bombardment which he expected to unleash on May 5, the Confederates slipped out of their entrenchments during the evening of May 3. The Federal command was caught off balance by this unexpected retreat. The Union soldiers were, however, jubilant that the siege was now over. Soldiers raced to win lasting glory by placing their unit's colors first atop the Confederate earthworks. Edward Wilson of Birney's Zouaves achieved this honor when he affixed the Stars and Stripes on the crest of the Lee's Mill battlements.

As the Federal soldiers entered the Confederate positions, they were shocked to discover the torpedoes left behind to retard their advance. Developed by Brigadier General Gabriel J. Rains, these land mines were actually 8- or 10-inch Columbiad shells buried a few inches under the soil and set with primers so that they exploded when stepped on or moved. It was the first use of this controversial weapon during the Civil War, and these buried shells injured scores of Union soldiers.

McClellan immediately ordered a pursuit, which was slowed by heavy rains and the land mines left by the Southerners. Union troops marched over the muddy roads, already rutted by the retreating Confederates, while frequently skirmishing with the Southerners.

The Union advance guard, cavalry, and horse artillery, commanded by Brigadier General George Stoneman, finally caught up to the Confederate rearguard near where the two main Peninsula roads converged on Williamsburg. The Southern cavalry, commanded by J.E.B. Stuart (pictured here), was under considerable pressure by the Union advance. As darkness began to shroud the crossroads and Federal infantry arrived on the scene, the Confederates were able to take refuge behind a series of redoubts that Magruder had built months before.

George McClellan spent much of May 4 in Yorktown organizing his pursuit. He hoped that by rushing Brigadier General William B. Franklin's division up the York River to Eltham's Landing, the Confederate army would be intercepted enroute to Richmond. The strike force moving to cut off the Confederate rearguard near Williamsburg was placed under the command of Brigadier General Edwin Vose "Bull" Sumner (pictured here).

Major General James Longstreet had been placed in command of the Confederate defense of the Williamsburg Line by General Joseph E. Johnston. Longstreet, in turn, ordered Brigadier General Richard Heron Anderson (pictured here) to hold the Confederate lines around Fort Magruder. Anderson had two brigades to thwart any Union advance.

At dawn on May 5, 1862, Brigadier General Joseph Hooker had his troops ready to assault Fort Magruder. The Union troops made little headway. The mud and fierce Confederate defense stymied the Federal advance. Longstreet sent more Confederate troops into the fray sensing an opportunity to achieve a stunning victory.

As the sound of the battle grew louder, Joe Johnston returned to Williamsburg to confer with "Old Pete" Longstreet (pictured here). The Confederates decided to seize the initiative and pressed the Federal left back toward the Hampton Road. By mid-afternoon, the Union troops were in danger of being flanked.

The battle began to turn in favor of the Union when Brigadier General Philip Kearny's division arrived from Yorktown. Around 4 pm, Kearny led his men into the fray shouting, "I am a one-armed Jersey son-of-a-gun, follow me!" Kearny personally reconnoitered the front and as each unit formed into line he announced, "Men, I want you to drive those black guards to hell at once." The troops surged forward and retook the captured Federal batteries. Soon the Confederates had fallen back on Fort Magruder and the line stabilized to the morning's positions.

Early in the afternoon "Bull" Sumner had learned from a contraband that the Confederate left was unprotected. Two redoubts were vacant, one of which guarded the important passage over the mill dam on Cub Creek (a tributary of Queens Creek). Sumner sent Brigadier General Winfield Scott Hancock to capture the redoubts. As Kearny prepared his attack, Hancock moved his troops virtually behind Fort Magruder and shelled the Confederate positions.

Longstreet had already committed all his troops into the action in front of Fort Magruder when he noticed the Federal flanking position on his left. He requested support from Major General D.H. Hill's division. Hill sent Brigadier General Jubal A. Early's brigade. Early commanded the left wing consisting of the 24th and 38th Virginia, while Hill (pictured here) led the 23rd and 5th North Carolina on the right.

The brigade marched into the dense woods toward the sound of Hancock's cannon fire. The units lost their alignment and direction as they struggled through the underbrush. Early and the 24th Virginia were the first to gain the clearing, but it was over 600 yards in front, rather than on the flank of the Union position. Early, instead of waiting for the rest of the brigade, wheeled his men about and marched toward the Federals.

The Confederates were hit with a telling fire. Jubal Early (pictured here) was shot through the shoulder and had to be removed from the field, faint from loss of blood, while urging his men onward. The Carolina regiments emerged onto the field and attempted to support the Virginians. Hill quickly ordered a halt to the "fatally destructive and disjointed assault." The Confederates suffered heavy casualties and fell back in rout.

117

McClellan called the Battle of Williamsburg "an accident" caused by too rapid a pursuit. The Confederates suffered 1,603 casualties, and the Federals, 2,239. "Hancock was superb," McClellan wired Washington, D.C. The Army of the Potomac had at last fought a major battle, and McClellan declared that "The victory is complete."

Joe Johnston had a different interpretation of the battle, as he later wrote, "Had the enemy beaten us on the fifth, as he claims to have done, our army would have lost most of its baggage and artillery." Though the Federals were able to force the Confederates to abandon Williamsburg, Longstreet's rearguard gave Johnston time to move his army toward Richmond.

Williamsburg was a mismanaged battle by
both commands. McClellan allowed the
Confederate army to once again escape his
grasp. The Union thrust against the retreating
Confederates did not end at Williamsburg.
McClellan had spent most of the day of
the battle supervising the embarkation of
Franklin's division onto transports to cut off
the Confederate retreat up the York River near
Eltham's Landing.

Brigadier General William B. Franklin's
(pictured here) division reached Eltham's
Landing on May 6. The Union troops
disembarked and entrenched under the
protection of Federal gunboats. Joe Johnston
reacted quickly to contain this threat by
sending Major General G.W. Smith's wing of
the Confederate army from Barhamsville to
Eltham's Landing. Smith ordered Brigadier
General William Whiting to press the
Federals and a brief attack ensued with minor
casualties. Whiting's attack secured the
Confederate flank and enabled Johnston's
army to continue its retreat to Richmond.

Abraham Lincoln was disenchanted with McClellan's progress up the Peninsula and decided to visit Fort Monroe so to prompt greater action. Lincoln arrived at Old Point Comfort on the evening of May 6, accompanied by Secretary of War Edwin Stanton and Secretary of Treasury Salmon Chase. Since the Confederate army was now in retreat toward Richmond, Lincoln immediately met with Major General John E. Wool and Flag Officer Louis N. Goldsborough to send his fleet to attack the Sewell's Point batteries the next day.

Around noon on May 8, the Union fleet, led by the *Monitor* and *Naugatuck*, began shelling Sewell's Point. Lincoln went to Fort Wool to observe the attack. Fort Wool's Sawyer and James rifles also joined in the bombardment until from behind Craney Island appeared the *Virginia*. The Confederate ironclad immediately steamed toward Sewell's Point, and the Federal ships retreated to the protection of Fort Monroe.

Lincoln was frustrated by this turn of events and ordered Wool to land his troops and then march toward Norfolk. Under cover of a naval bombardment, the Union troops landed at Ocean View on May 9 and began their march to town. The Confederates evacuated Norfolk, Portsmouth, and the Gosport Navy Yard as the Union army approached.

When the Confederates abandoned the Gosport Navy Yard, the C.S.S. *Virginia* was left without a base. The Confederate ironclad could not be moved to Richmond because of its deep draught. The *Virginia* was run aground off Craney Island, and around 4:30 am on the morning of May 11, the vessel was destroyed by her crew. Chief Engineer Asthon Ramsay reflected, "Still unconquered, we hauled down our drooping colors . . . and with mingled pride and grief gave her to the flames."

The *Virginia's* destruction opened the James River to the Union fleet. The U.S. Navy immediately sent the ironclads *Monitor* and *Galena* (pictured here) with three other ships up the James River. The Confederates, realizing this threat to Richmond, installed heavy guns at Fort Darling on Drewry's Bluff and sank stone-laden barges in the river channel as obstructions. When the Federal ships approached Drewry's Bluff on May 15, 1862, neither ironclad could elevate their guns to fire at the batteries on the bluff. The *Galena* was severely damaged during the engagement and the Union vessels were forced to retreat.

The U.S.S. *Monitor* played a minor role in the Drewry's Bluff engagement. The *Monitor* spent the remainder of the summer in Hampton Roads before undergoing repairs in the Washington Navy Yard. Late in November the ironclad returned to Hampton. On December 30, 1862, while enroute to South Carolina under the tow of the U.S.S. *Rhode Island*, the *Monitor* foundered in a storm off Cape Hatteras with the loss of four officers and twelve men.

Nine

Occupation and Surrender

The Confederacy never gave up hope of liberating Hampton Roads, but the constant pressure on Richmond by the Federal army left it unable to make any concerted effort. As with the transformation of the steam frigate *Merrimack* into the ironclad *Virginia*, the Confederacy strove to use its limited resources to undermine the Union occupation. The C.S.S. *Squib* is one such case. The *Squib* was a steam launch built in Richmond featuring a spar torpedo and commanded by Lieutenant Hunter Davidson, C.S.N., who served on the *Virginia*.

In the early morning of April 9, 1864, Davidson steered the *Squib* through the entire Union fleet and exploded a torpedo against the Federal flagship U.S.S. *Minnesota* off Newport News Point. Despite the heavy gunfire brought against his little vessel, Davidson was able to escape. The torpedo's 53 pounds of powder did minor damage to the *Minnesota*'s hull. The *Squib* made another attempt on April 11, but the Federals were now alert to this threat and ran the launch off with cannon fire.

The James River was the final stage of yet another naval drama, the sinking of the C.S.S. *Florida* on November 28, 1864. The *Florida* was one of several vessels constructed in British shipyards for the Confederacy. John Newland Maffitt, a pre-war Warwick County resident, took command of the ship in the Bahamas and led the *Florida* on a highly successful cruise during 1863. Under Maffitt's eight-month command, the *Florida* and her satellites captured forty-seven Northern vessels.

Maffitt became too ill to continue as the *Florida*'s captain and was replaced by Lieutenant Charles N. Morris. The highly successful commerce raider's career soon ended when she was rammed and captured by the U.S.S. *Wachusett* in Bahia, Brazil. Although this act was a violation of Brazilian neutrality, the *Wachusett* towed the *Florida* to Hampton Roads. When Brazil demanded the *Florida*'s return, Rear Admiral David Porter, commander of the North Atlantic Blockading Squadron, ordered "that Rebel vessel" to be sunk. On November 28, 1864, the *Florida* quietly sank off Newport News Point after a "collision" with another vessel.

The Peninsula continued to serve as an important base for Union operations in Virginia and along the Southern coast. The 1863 Suffolk Campaign, Ben Butler's failed Bermuda Hundred Campaign, and the amphibious assault on Fort Fisher were launched from Fort Monroe. Fort Fisher guarded Wilmington, North Carolina, and the Union capture of this port sealed off the Confederacy from European supplies. It was virtually the end for the Confederacy.

A final effort to resolve the war to obtain a mediated peace was held on February 3, 1865, aboard the steamer *River Queen* off Old Point Comfort. The Hampton Roads Peace Conference proved to be a total failure. The war was destined to go on until its bloody end, which soon came on April 9, 1865. Even after the war's conclusion, the Peninsula continued to serve the victorious Union army. A prison camp was built on Newport News Point, next to Camp Butler, to house the thousands of captured Confederates. This effort proved futile and the Newport News POW Camp closed in August 1865.

One prisoner did remain incarcerated on the Peninsula, the former Confederate president Jefferson Davis. Davis was held captive at Fort Monroe under the strictest guard and regulations, as he was charged with treason as well as being implicated in Lincoln's assassination. A casemate was initially used to hold Davis, but his declining health prompted Federal officials to better his quarters. Jefferson Davis was released on bail ($100,000) on May 13, 1867.

126

Keith Curtis was born in 1844. County native, he attended ̣aytop Cary's Hampton Military ̣emy. Curtis enlisted in the Old ̣ninion Dragoons (Co. B, 3rd ̣rginia Cavalry) on October 6, 1861, and was wounded in the elbow by a gunshot at Funkstown, Maryland, during the Gettysburg Campaign. Promoted to sergeant, Curtis served with his unit until the war's end.

Curtis returned home after the war to find a wasteland. "Where once a modest cottage sheltered the farmer and growing family, a ruined chimney, like a smoked skeleton, haunted the farm," wrote W.H.T. Squires, "Poverty, wretchedness, hunger, death and despair clutched the heart of the land." Curtis, who later served as sheriff of Elizabeth City County, was one of many veterans who worked to rebuild the Peninsula community in the post-war era. By the time of his death in 1913, Robert Keith Curtis had witnessed a major transformation: where once there was peaceful farmland, two new cities had grown out of the ashes of war.

Acknowledgments

I am indebted to several individuals whose efforts made this important collection of images available for publication. As with previous projects, I must thank my wife, Martha, for typing my text and offering much-needed moral support. Of course, my son, John Moran, must be lauded for all of his patience. Fellow Virginia War Museum colleagues J. Michael Moore and Sarah Goldberger collected period line art and photographs from various public institutions. In addition, J. Michael Moore organized this collection for publication. Tim Smith, a Virginia War Museum board member, also collected images from private sources and donated his considerable photographic talents to this project.

The following individuals aided the photographic editors and myself: Audrey C. Johnson of the Library of Virginia and Ann-Marie Price at the Virginia Historical Society found many rare images of the Virginia Peninsula; David Johnson of the Casemate Museum loaned us many rare photographs of Fort Monroe, Fort Wool, and the Peninsula; Karl Sundstrom granted us permission to use two rare photographs of the Chesapeake and Hampton Military Hospitals from his personal collection; Paul A. Carnahan at the Vermont Historical Society permitted the usage of the George Houghton photographs of the Peninsula Campaign; and Michael Cobb of the City of Hampton spent countless hours finding antebellum images of Elizabeth City County and Hampton.

Photo Credits